# TRANSITION TO PHILOSOPHY VOLUME TWO

*JOHANNES BERGFORS*

**chipmunkapublishing**
the mental health publisher

All rights reserved, no part of this publication may be reproduced by any means, electronic, mechanical photocopying, documentary, film or in any other format without prior written permission of the publisher.

>Published by
>Chipmunkapublishing
>United Kingdom

**http://www.chipmunkapublishing.com**

Copyright © JOHANNES BERGFORS 2025

# TRANSITION TO PHILOSOPHY VOLUME TWO

# JOHANNES BERGFORS

\<BEE\>



My brother goes out for kebabs. How can I talk of him without mentioning his philosophy all over? He says <BEE> might soon ensue from @ in the international language alphabet. It is thus in his credo. As I stated in *Transition to Philosophy* he designed an experiment with more than one bit of paper, containing diagrams, which contain the idea mentioned. He is now the boss of the art dealing company, partly because of my illness, partly because of his genius. As I said in *Transition To Philosophy* <BEE> is the only original idea in it. Be free, <BEE>, when you sail across the sea! I think of Wittgenstein who seems at times to be pertaining towards a more international lexicon. My brother produced evidence of it. I think in <BEE> we all agree that something good has been uttered. I think we are united in blessing <BEE>. As I stated in *Transition To Philosophy* <BEE> could be a mode to drift off on. So we see that in the end it is my own brother who is the one to deliver us from all evil. He said the way his computer broke "wasn't the Feds." That "the Feds had nothing to do with it. It was cheap equipment." He is trying to fix it, get new parts shipped in. He is delivering my kebab back from Millom. I said in *Transition* I would do whatever James wants to do with his <BEE> even if it be maintain a philosophical silence but things have gone on. I wonder if doing anything other than <BEE> appears evil in a relative way. I don't know what to say now – at the impasse – but he's done it to turn us on. He gets back with the kebab. He's had a bad day. But I'm sure he'll be able to fix his computer. As he says "we live in hope."



Although that could be a good place to leave it for now I have little else to do but try and "get philosophical" about my brother's burp. He burped when he got home. One sense of this utterance is that my own philosophy, compared with <BEE> is but a shameless belly burp. But there are other meanings I feel too tired to strive for. The inverse meaning is immediately upon me: that his philosophy is a burp or rather that we are to interpret the burp *in the context* of his philosophy not mine. If you think satire's leaking in that is not intentional. In the context of James's philosophy, you find the burp in realtime no different from another burp, but in reflection, in afterthought, in aftertaste, a far more meaningful burp. When I say "meaningful" that is measured against meaning as we once knew it; and yet with <BEE> around, values need tearing down and erecting anew. Indeed that is exactly what <BEE> is about and James himself cites Nietzsche as an influence. He's a philosophical genius that leaves me feeling "abstracted from knowledge."

## FRAGMENTS FROM THE DIARY OF A PHILOSOPHER

3.

It's a new day now, and already the evening. I spent the day mostly washing up. James's computer part arrived but he couldn't get his novel back. I myself had to move on from a diary, a diary, if you can believe it, because Mr. Yellow had a McHappy day again, eh? I'm quite glad too, because in <BEE> we have something precious, and it should come at the start not the end. I can't tell you why I am not free to write a diary in my own home, but not wanting any trouble, can but abide by the stringent system even if it seems stringent. One thing I can try and do is ship in bits from the diary, bits that are less than contentious.

4.


But living in the sticks with mental illness is awful... should I set up a Republic with pollen as a currency? I think my dad tried it one summer! But now there is no more pollen, not anymore... indeed, the pollen has gone under Gondwanaland, the ecstasy pill gone under the green hill.

5.

So I am watching a Youtube video about Socratic method.

I learn of the Ancient Greek word *nous* (pronounced "noose").

It means the Great Mind that orders things.

I start to wonder if it is the origin of the demotic word for "nous" (pronounced "nowse") as in "if he had any nous about him he wouldn't have done that."

English is already jumbled, polyglot, inbred, cross-pollinated, mongrelised, higgledy-piggledy. They say the streets of London are the same; where in France where you have le and la everything is more ordered, which in turn reflects the geography of Paris.

I believe Paris was lucky enough to escape getting bombed in the war.

Speaking of war I read an article on the war Russia is waging against Ukraine. The German guy Merz has announced that restrictions on the range of Ukrainian missiles have been scrapped.

6.

Now it's the end of the day – 21. 22.

I mentioned in an earlier draft of *Transition To Philosophy* a feeling of butterflies in my stomach when waking on a Saturday morning in London.

Up here it's more about the fleeting, evocative light at the end of a summer day, almost calling to you from over the fell.

It gives you that strange tingly sensation.

Here would be a great place to smoke pollen.

The sunset comes in synaesthetic ways – it is a perfumed sunset unto the young poet.

Now all light recedes to a vanishing point.

We look through the fingers of the dark trees in the foreground.

7.

It seems a bit prissy to be contemplating an MA when there is war in the world.

Those that returned from the Second World War just never spoke about it.

Now we've got war in both Ukraine and the Gaza Strip.

Sometimes I feel that with my CV, I should be guided in designing a new World Order, a plan for a shock-proof world.

At 7 I helped invent the net, at 8 was the witness from Jim Morrison's book, *The Lords And The New Creatures*, twice. At 11 I was marked on the hand by an experiment into the maths of the new colour as a cellular mark. At 15 I attained the face of stars which was scripted in the Bible. At 18 I forewarned of September 11th and wrote the highest-marked A-level exam essay in the nation at 100%.

After leaving school, I recorded an album on binaural earphones, hosted the Plough alignment for a rhythm change in the White House, got a First, worked at a numinous, purple-bleeding screen, built the Tower as an object of philosophy, had an experiment into a tape with a pause where resealed in the flimsy reel, and when my dad died I discovered the sheet where pictures grew.

It strikes me that the trajectory of my life is analogous to John Barnes's sensational goal against Brazil, beating player after player.

It strikes me that the discovery of the sheet is analogous to the ball ending up in the back of the net after a long, mazy run that incorporated all those moves I made.

This is why I think I should be guided in designing a shock-proof world.

Before you say I was greedy, I never earned 1p throughout.

But I would agree that only one of those things would normally be enough.

It even becomes a strain to get through, a rigmarole, what with there being so many things to impart and so I just skim the surface as above.

8.

Wittgenstein said a lot of pain was caused by misunderstanding because we misunderstood the logic of our language and he hoped to clarify things.

I went back to bed and slept a long time and woke again at around 7 PM, thinking about communication, problems understanding the logic of our language.

At 12 I had a complete emotional collapse in the I. T. Room at prep school, and when the teacher was asking and asking "what's wrong? What's wrong?" all I could say was "I don't know! I don't know!"

I think I lacked the tools for talking about what had happened – which at that stage was only a certain way into my story.

It's fitting that it was the I. T. room because as I have said at 7 I helped invent the net and the only problem with that was that the book had to be stored in the attic for as long as my father lived… for someone needed to store the idea of the net in writing in the attic to give it a chance to bloom. That was not the problem.

The problem was partly that at 8 I was twice, twice made the witness from Jim Morrison's book *The Lords And The New Creatures*.

Then by 11 I was marked on the hand by an experiment into the maths of the new colour as a cellular mark that was contained in the net book in the attic unbeknownst to me.

This was when I broke down in the I. T. Room, had the emotional collapse.

As you can imagine I lacked the tools for discussion.

The terms on which discussion could be held were over my head and out of my reach.

I now think *The Lords And The New Creatures*, Jim Morrison's book, was realised as part of my dad's business – and meanwhile he told us his business was something else.

I had to reach the age of 43 before the confusion was cleared up. In many ways now I have the ability to talk about it, I am told I mustn't.

**9.**

Two cups equal in size occupy the table. For me to know they are equal in size I must have a preconceived notion of equality that comes before the physical, material world of forms. It is a priori and preceding sense-perception.

Similarly Wittgenstein says in the sentences "Here is a red patch" and "here there isn't a red patch" the word red occurs in both so cannot indicate the presence of something red.

**10.**

Tonight there is no "Silken Veil" effect. The "Silken Veil" effect, once again is when the dying light calls to you, beckons to you, with piercing clarity, from over the shoulder of the darkened fell, at the end of day.

I used to call the top of Sea Ness "the alien spaceship landing site," when the 4 of us went up to play.

It is not just the poet that renames reality like a myth-maker though, for philosophers often set about Christening their word-worlds too.

I heard that the foothill Sea Ness used to be Seer Ness after a seer and his trance.

The locals now know me as a seer because of things I have seen in terms of animals, constellations and the future as well.

Tonight I can report that it's not the right weather for the Silken Veil effect.

Darkness descends; and yet what is in that expression but a cliché from the cinema?

I sit and drink tea – is that where it begins?

Another idea I had – albeit when stoned – was to set up a third House of Parliament called "The House of New Creatures" – after Jim Morrison's book – and make it here – where not only did we have the new creatures dream realised so to speak – but where the stars re-align.

My mum would go ape because "this is a private residence," as the Dude says in the film *The Big Lebowski*.

Well, films. Everything in a film is deliberate which is why it was wrong of them to start making changes to Morrison's thesis on film aesthetics, *The Lords*.

Film can be about narrative, but also about immersion in the liquid dream.

My favourite films include *Pi, Requiem For A Dream, The Big Lebowski, The Doors, Lawrence of Arabia, A Beautiful Mind, Fight Club, Eraserhead, The Warriors, La Heine,* and much of Tarantino too.

They seem a motley and disparate crew, incongruous with each other.

I forgot to mention *Withnail and I*, also *The Empire Strikes Back*.

As for my favourite books, it's a difficult question but I would have to say at the moment: *Paradise Lost, The Four Quartets, Ulysses, The Lords And The New Creatures, A Season In Hell, On The Road, A Confederacy of Dunces, Crow, The Hippopotamus, Tractatus Logico-Philosophicus, Philosophical Investigations, The Beach, Selected Poems* by Michael Hofmann, anything by the New York School of poets, and that's all that comes to mind right now.

My favourite albums include *OK Computer, Nevermind,* The first Doors album, *Piper At the Gates of Dawn, Music Has The Right To Children, Kid A, Drukqs* by Aphex Twin, *Ten* by Pearl Jam, *16 Stone* by Bush, *Surfer Rosa* by The Pixies, and more and many more.

I hear Pulp – the Britpop band from the 1990's – are getting back together and that's a good thing to see. My first LSD trip was spent watching Pulp headline Glastonbury and they were electric, absolutely amazeballs.

Now I am thinking of a happier time, when I was young, attractive, free, not yet a failure, not yet mentally ill – and when we had the London house as well.


I forgot to mention in the films *Waking Life* and *A Scanner Darkly*.


They both seem to unite narrative and immersion into one.

**11.**

I do some more reading, remember the time my friend "Agent G" said to wtire aoubt planiyg the panio uisng the scablmre teuqinhce – where you rearrange all the letters of a word apart from the first and last and the eye can still tell what is being said.

I liad my fregnis dwon on the agnteemud fftih, (for eamplxe).

With a palindrome I wouldn't do it.

I've also got quite a collection of stress-relieving acid-casualty doodles, that in my "system" are "letters." Some people think the doodles my best work! Others contend it was when I made the Nirvana barcode to be but the beat of 'Scentless Apprentice' by Nirvana tapped out in approximate barcode shape using the tool of the qwerty keyboard:

|| | |||| | || | ||||     909 & 693 are wings

Literature is the ultimate function of my life. Literature is its sole purpose. To take away my literature would be wrong, even if as some have decreed it with a pathological and nosological eye, my continued writing is out of illness.

**12.**

In bed, at night, I consider the idea that they can manipulate the stars, but who? Who gave us the face of stars? I mean was it aliens or was it the early Christians who encrypted it in the Bible?

I also consider the gap. In an earlier draft of *Transition To Philosophy* I mentioned that there is a large "gap" between being a species descended from cannibals, and the elegance and order in the universe that is shown by the Plough alignment as concurred with a rhythm change in the White House. Thinking about the gap is staggering and might entail redefining metaphysics. I heard metaphysics previously described as "the place where science and religion meet."

About the face I believe it was scripted by early Christians, but that isn't to say there is no possibility of alien life-forms.

About the gap I muse deep and long. The gap between a once-barbaric species and the elegance of the re-alignment is massive.

I'm also doing my best to try and forgive and forget about the way I was treated w/r/t being cursed or worse hypnotised.

I hope I would be treated with the same forgiveness.

As for the gap, the universe is a very mysterious place and it could be that uncertainty will always prevail when it comes to unravelling those mysteries.

For when they talk about "progress" or "getting closer to the point" or "syncretism" or "logical positivism" that Bigger Picture to which things tend could be the alignment itself.

The dimensions are inch perfect.

It is not a vision unlike the face of stars for it combines already-existing things into something like the sum of all difference connected.

It is nearer Sigma from maths than a vision.

**13.**

When we were but kids, young kids, living in London, a new cartoon came on telly, with two bears of different colouration talking in English accents on some moon-like out-post or space station maybe, at night. Their conversation was deep and humourous too and my mother told me it was a new series.

The next week I came back to the telly to look for it again but it was gone. It was a one off. It was even a brain-trick. What it taught us I don't know but maybe that life is more important than telly. I think of those two bears now that my brother and I are without other company out here at reality's starry faultline, on the edge of Night.

**14.**

And to those that say I have surrendered my sense-perception to a kind of prostitution in becoming such a witness to so many things what do I retort?

Do I not say it's been character-building?

Do I not maintain that such perceptions are special unlike the relationship you have with an actual prostitute?

Was I not the key witness for the whole counter-cultural Revolution?

**15.**

"Does a thought move or does it just happen?" I asked my friend, when we were undergraduates and he said "it's a good question." Poetry was broken in that time succeeding September 11$^{th}$. Some of us had to go to University in 2002 as proven prophets – or rather I did. But I was ignorant of my own prophecy, through cannabis, until a few years later. Now I read Wittgenstein, detecting mild undertones, maybe even "hidden meanings" beneath the Euclidean word-surface.

(This only reminds me of a school I was at where they called me the Human Dictionary and got me to talk about the hidden meaning of a spoon.)

"Does a thought move or does a thought just happen?" Well, a question is an Access All Areas card in the Great Unknown. The spirit of Modernism is the spirit of inquiry. Uncertainty is alive. Sartre says (what does Sartre say?) something about how a question implies the fact of negation (or maybe it was the other way round.) I want to make philosophy as good as the movies. That is my new tentatively stated ambition at the laptop. So far I'd say *Tractatus* is better than Proust.

# JOHANNES BERGFORS

16.


The history of philosophy – its early years – are the same whether or not you read about it in Bertrand Russell's *History of Western Philosophy* from 1961 or you watch a Youtube video, showing a series of lectures recorded in the 1990's in an American University. The same names and motifs crop up. Thales is mentioned at the start, who predicted an eclipse, meaning science and philosophy started at the same time. Having predicted several things successfully, my CV thus lends me to philosophy, where James is more the type of intellectual who has the creative edge. I also predicted the hunt for the God Particle the same year as I did September 11$^{th;}$ which reminds me of Democritus of the Ancient Greeks who said atoms in the soul are as dust motes in a ray of light when there is no wind. For it was looking at a ballet of dust in a late ray of light angling in that I made the God Particle prophecy!

I since read in a book of Physics that the idea of the God Particle is daft. I never said it wasn't, only that they would begin to look for it as if God were not extrinsic to matter.

Matter is only semi-state.

Everything in Nature is too.

Everything is shifting, changing, temporal, in flux, even the oldest fell; but philosophers still believe in a kind of truth that is fixed, eternal, static and timeless!

This does not mean "relative" truth but the opposite!

I consider now whether the idea that "there is no such thing as mind cancer" is but a relative truth or timeless and universal.

*****

**17.**


At 05. 48, I think to note down the time for a change, and to stop doing it in the future too. I was going to say as well EVERYTHING IN THIS TEXT GOES ON IN THE HAPPY WORLD OF HARIBO. But who would understand in 20, 000 years when my text has superseded the Bible!? If the Haribo comment comes from my lovely sister Hannah, there is a Dr. Bob comment too: he says to include the line ALL OF A SUDDEN CAIN PULLED OUT A GUN AND KILLED ABEL. For then you have a story. But mentioning these things only reminds me of what I was thinking about there being no such thing as mind-cancer – which I was about to declare as at bottom sterile, and then further, declare falsifiable – but through falsifiability there is no 100% truth, only the best theory at the time. It is through poetry and its sensibility of truth-to-itself that a proposition can be 100% if well-made enough. So I wonder which of the two the proposition counts as.

18.

We come to a work presupposing binary oppositions, some of which might incorporate:

narrative/ confessional;

honesty/ craft;

inside/ outside a convention;

art/ science;

**high-end/ low-end;**

**and a good work, whatever genre or mode of writing it is, can undo these binary oppositions, open new fields of language.**

19.

There is a large, old-fashioned painting in the posh, coffee-cake dining room with a large, ornate frame; and in the painting you can see God's nostril encrypted in a stylish way into the grey cloud-scape; and it is only upon noticing this detail transmitted down the years correctly that when you next come back to the painting it has become 4D and is suddenly alive with colour even though it still bears the grey semblance of its ostensible surfaces.

**20.**

I am thinking of the bit in literature when Henry Miller and his mate cut up Spinoza and put it in the teapot. Later, moving rooms, I think again of the way a new supercomputer can put every word, book, sentence, letter, paragraph in every order. Even *Tractatus Logico-Philosophicus* is prefigured, or would be if it were being made anew; and attempts to make new things in this day and age are all prefigured, foreseen.

The rain has stopped freckling the patio.

The wind is rustling in the trees.


Cloud covers the fell still.


A bird is calling out the front.


I don't want to finish a follow up soon but take my time and cement a position, develop a stance.


What does dad mean when he says "Order is Happiness" and what when he says "life is one?"


I look out the window at the green tree swaying, ask myself "do you see God in that tree?" and see none, then try and superimpose God onto it, like a template, but it won't work. It is a prettier sight, nevertheless, than real live death on the morning news.


The tree inveigles the super-involuted structure of the eye.


Sometimes I think of sex as an evolutionary corridor down which you can stare to the elemental realms, the religion of anima...

sometimes I stare through linear light at the tree.


It is waving not drowning.


Sometimes through purple germs accrued in aleatory patterns on the window's big, oblong, staring eye I look and see the tree undress, and how in Infinity there is no difference between, say, "tree" and "tarantula," nor are they on a different scale.


The tree's new green-ness is refreshing for the eye; and the bird song is going mad like John Coltrane.


Now I will wait for future time.


Now it is future time.


Now I am a philosopher there is little else to do but read and think. I stare in a long, golden trance at the tree outside the window and notice by means of description that its leafy boughs seem in the wind to be bouncing a basketball, or stroking a cat.


I close my eyes and my mind fills with light then I open them again and realise it's the literal light of day coming through the window.

I sit and contemplate more, how Jesus would say to forgive the guy that cursed or worse hypnotised you.


My mind drifts off to free-range running and bracken I. D. cards, out of sight out of mind to the powers that be. When I am back in the room the name of the game is Logic. I can think of two senses of Logic, two theories if you like:


1. that the number 1 is inferior to the number 2.


2. that the number 2 is inferior to the number 1.


The problem with writing a book about Logic is that it has to keep getting better and better aesthetically. So the first theory states 1 is inferior to 2, and everything is progressing logically; but then you start to ask of increased room for error, dissipation, entropy, weakness, dilution, and that the number 1 is that number to which all systems pertain. Because ultimately "life IS one" and "we are of ONE MIND." I hope we get through these dirty waters soon!


The first proposition is illogical in indicating that 1 is inferior to 2 in a qualitative way if 1 is hierarchically above it in the pecking order.

Of course in a quantitative way it is true.


The second is illogical too, at least in a quantitative way.


I hope we get through these dirty waters soon!


And did you know the decimal numbers of Pi are infinite?


And did you know Sigma is the sum of all data?


And now I stare at the tree again as if in a present tense sharpened and rinsed by flagrant flame!


And did you know dog = pi times Mc squared?


And O is the key of the babbling unicorn?


Logic again. If it were a clock, 1 would be inferior to 2, logically speaking, because logic implies that things are getting better. If it were a process of narrowing down or elimination towards a goal, 1 would be better than 2. I think here of love, of the idea that were are meant to settle on another soul and die alone. So there is room for both truths dependent on their context, meaning and use. So we must open what I call "A Quantum Field of Intelligence." Such a field is opened when, for example, something exists one minute and the next minute can't be found, or is made to look like a hoax but still exist in meaning. And here I sit waiting for the depot feeling exhausted and nervous at once.

## ON BEING SERVED THE BLOT TO WRITE ABOUT

It could be a mixture of Blur and Oasis, the big, black blot I put on the page:

●

My first work of philosophy, *Transition To Philosophy*, isn't even out there yet; and already I am thinking of a second, all about the blot.

When I studied Creative Writing at Warwick University we had an open-air poetry assignment, so as to not divorce poetry from its etymological origins *poesis* meaning "something which is brought into being."

Some hung strips of poetry from the trees, someone put a banner saying CRE before the sign for carpark 8, to make the word CRE8. Someone did something with a goldfish bowl. I myself at the time, with a friend, went on a roof to arrange an unused pile of bricks into the words: "PLANNING PERMISSION: BUILD PYRAMIDS OF NEW FOUND LAND."

And someone brought in a single full stop on a page entitled Writer's Block. I am not trying to rip him off herein, more write a book of philosophy.

Brian Patten, a poet I once admired greatly, said "death is the only grammatically correct full stop." Look at the sign. Analyse it. What does it say? What does it mean? Imagine if I had followed it up, or you had, by saying "yes indeed!"

Already I see a celebration of oddness; and then I think about Man's predicament on earth – how weird everything is, society bounding in circles round the sun – this prisoner planet, as my dad called it, where the answer may well be self-punishment.

Blur and Oasis meanwhile were both pretty good. Blur had the rhythm of attack you get from London, present in many of their bands like the Sex Pistols, the Rolling Stones, The Kinks, The Clash, Madness. You get it from the markets on the streets. Oasis meanwhile were characterised more by bittersweet, comedown energy. If they are married in the blot so be it, but that could be reading meaning in where there is none, with hermeneutic autonomy.

If Deconstruction is a dream, letting the eye become distracted by things not meant to be in the text, the monster learning the language in the hut in *Frankenstein* is Caliban from *The Tempest*.

Already you can see most of my education was in English and Creative Writing, not Philosophy.

Already, the blot is an imperfection; already a solar eclipse to look at; already it is difficult to pin down what I feel about the blot in words. To isolate, to say with pinpoint precision. Already in turn it means just that – the pinning down of something – but what?

The blot is the blot is the blot is the blot.

I believe I have seen it before, maybe in Wittgenstein.

Shall we revisit the microcosm, the atemporal isle, posit the blot all over? At some point I should, and what if it were blue and what if it were red? Can you "read" it? Or is there a difference between a simple shape and a line of meaning? It could be about someone that needs to stop writing and can't. I've been through 1000's of files. I've had 1000's of bright ideas. One of them was Action Thriller: to write an action thriller and cut it up and copy and paste it in a random fashion at the screen like Jackson Pollock making an action painting, and still calling it "Action Thriller." Chance collocations thus churn up evidence through the operation of a game. But now I am settling on philosophy. I felt apart from a few typos my first work in this field went quite well. No, I don't feel it is the former work that is the blot on the landscape.

My life went wrong with LSD and then I fluffed my Oxford interview. Could that be it? The meaning of the blot? You start to see it can be unpacked in several ways, that there is liberty in the mind. Even when the mind is stained by LSD you can replace with happy memories, positive self-message, log on your brain in the morning with fruit before you insufflate the fume of the Vape pen.

\*\*\*\*\*\*\*\*

What sound does the blot have? Isn't it strange how all it takes is a blot and everything can start to pour forth? I got it in a co-imaginative way: an old friend on magic alphabet radio: he said to write a second book of philosophy, when I can, about the blot. Thank you friend! So it is that I too sing the song of my self and my soul! I stand atop my Mnt Oblivion and fart out of the wrong orifice!

Let's say all the action, all the plot, goes on inside the blot. The blot is the plot or even the anti-plot. So what exactly happened? Did two youths board a train not knowing where it was headed in the middle of the Night in London? For a dare? For a probing of the edges of freedom? If we say they did, we now know where they ended up: the blot. So all the foci and loci of their voyage got compressed, concentrated into a singular motif.

The unity of everything under the sun; the way we are all of one mind: is this what I mean? I looked at my old, obsolete FB account the other day and found I had written a poem going:


if e = mc squ@red


c over G = ½


@ltern@tively put:


if e – mc squ@red = [0/ only rel@tive 0]


c over G = ½


@ltern@tively put:


if e – mc squ@red = [0/ only rel@tive 0]


c over G = ½


& life is 1

\*\*\*\*\*\*\*\*

That was when my letter 'a' function was broken. And how shall we relate the blot to the letter 'a' knowing 'a' comes first in the alphabet and there is only one blot? I now put one teabag in one cup and stir in the artificial sweetener with one spoon. I said already in *Transition To Philosophy* that we start with a playground full of friends, slowly discard them, settle on another soul and die alone.

\*\*\*\*\*\*\*\*

My friend who commissioned me to do this, he knows what he wants and goes for it: is very singular in his tastes and passions. Yet if you only like, say, The Clash, and never broaden your taste, how can you even be said to like music at all? Speaking of music: I had a cassette tape of Pearl Jam 'VS' that had a pause where the flimsy reel was cut and resealed. The ideal was to do away with the pause, even to create a poetry machine in perpetual motion.

It worked; the pause was done away with. I thought I'd mention this because I was talking at the time about E pi E as a word pronounced "ette" and that roundness reminds of the blot. Should I posit the blot again or not posit the blot? Without thinking about what's gone into it, I already knew I was going to posit it twice. You get some people who posit a blank page for example: I did that in the school poetry mag. They said it was "second to none." Now the blot that can be unpacked in sooooooo many ways:

●

It's not as big as last time. What could be in it? No thought was put into it. It could be a spatio-temporal context. Here is my Walden, all apart from the deep, green bassoon.

About Blur and Oasis merged: one had a song called Coffee And TV, the other Cigarettes and Alcohol. It was drinking coffee and smoking cigarettes one day in the shed where I first conceived of the blot as a mixture of Blur and Oasis. That was long ago. I don't smoke cigarettes anymore. Anyhow, Wittgenstein says language conveys a picture in the mind: is the blot a picture?

I went down to a festival celebrating the solar eclipse with P, and we took too much LSD on the night before the eclipse. It was Lucy in the soul with demons whom as I have said elsewhere might happen to be an actual substance. On the day of the actual eclipse, the weather was grey and got greyer. Nobody needed the X-ray specs because the sun was obscured by cloud. Waking that morning, the day of the eclipse, after the dark night of the soul before it, I felt strangely empty, as if I had lost contact with myself. I was as Syd Barrett sang on The Madcap Laughs "alone and unreal." But here I am. Here is my Walden, minus the deep, green bassoon.

There is an effect here that is like "The Silken Veil." I call it "The Silken Veil Effect." It's when distant, fading light, of piercing lucidity, calls to you from o'er the shoulder of the fell at sundown, when the fell in the foreground is black and you can just see the fading light. It is around that time now but grey clouds have obscured the sky.

Soon I might be on the lookout for the moon.

In fact going out there is a patch of purple cloud-mountains – an enchanted kingdom – to the left of the fell - and the moon burns bright but is not spherical. And so we reach the end of another day. Yesterday's writing is still on my mind. Tomorrow I might fit it in. Today is where we live, tonight, tonight.

As a teenage philosopher I drew two, large, overlapping circles, one for the Known, one for the Unknown, and said the small, oval-shaped bit in the middle where they overlapped and clapped was "the area of self." The idea was that the circles grow together. As the Unknown becomes the Known the area of self in the middle subsumes both the circles into one. There is a total eclipse.

# JOHANNES BERGFORS

*****

Last night I was awake all night. I loaned the idea for writing a new book of philosophy about "the blot" from the air – an old friend in the network of voices. I walked around the kitchen postponing it, thinking about the war, how terrible it is. I actually wrote a poem, the first for a long time, in the night-time:

This broken clock impression

is getting quite good -

up all night, walking

in a circle round the kitchen.

It's the second night in a row.

There is war in the world.

Grizzly war, Hellish war,

painful war, colourful & loud.

And what good can a writer do?

But affect incremental changes?

I walk in darkness around

this kitchen – apart from voices.


In my mind a meerkat

attacks a deadly snake.

In an aggressive burst of energy.

O send us the light, Dear Lord.



\*\*\*\*\*\*\*\*



I didn't think it was a bad poem, and it probably led me to fiddling with poem files again. By daybreak I was so tired I couldn't sleep and got a sleeping pill from James. Today I got up late, and we had a Take-away pizza, and I then set about working on my new philosophy book, all about the blot. I forgot to mention that at some point yesterday, before the sleeping pill, I actually read *Transition To Philosophy* and thought it wasn't that bad. Often writers don't get round to reading their own work but I did. One problem was that it didn't really try and stop the war! That was what I mostly noticed! So I wrote a little poem yesterday – and today woke up and got busy with the blot. The blot is now the plot! It has already been contended by the air's mind that my writing about the blot is more thoughtful than my other writing. Every full stop could be the blot in disguise. Is the blot not about how philosophy is a self-contained language corresponding to nothing real in life?

\*\*\*\*\*\*\*\*

Now it is later. It is past midnight again. Maybe the idea of the blot – of writing about the blot – was not meant to be a generative device but to get me to stop? Or maybe to get me to try and stop the war? The world is an uneasy place at the moment, as you can tell even up here in a world of Romantic escape. I feel uneasy and turn to Wittgenstein. Maybe to know your own philosophy you must first know who your favourite philosopher is? Similarly to unpack something that happens in your own country, even if it is to do with an American media-compression experiment, you may have to read some indigenous philosophy. And when your mate's dad says to you in the pub "when you get old your body starts to hurt," is that not philosophy by means of it pertaining to being axiomatic, truthful, or is philosophy something more than that, something analytic, something transcendent, something to do with suspension of judgement, or ecstasia, and a process of clarification, a teasing out of arguments, a resistance to preaching, to sermonisation, but a dissection of language, culture, meaning… what does philosophy mean to you and why? And then it is the same for the blot. Not "what does the blot mean?" but "what does the blot mean for you and why?" The blot is not universal in meaning like God just because it contains an absence of meaning-signifiers. It is surely subjective in meaning even though it contains an absence of meaning-signifiers. And as I stated in an earlier draft of *Transition To Philosophy*, "we must have the Right to Disagree," like Lennon getting high in his tree. If the blot is an aperture, for example, is it closed to you and open to someone else? If it is a picture of an astral body unto one person, is it the singularity of a black hole unto another? And what would Mr. Bean, who delivered a lecture on art at the end of the Bean Movie, make of the blot as a work of art? Is it my "God is dead" moment – in the sense that meaning has grown diverted? Or is it more Duchamp? And when I say it contains an absence of meaning-signifiers, is that even true? Do I mean it? Or is there in that absence itself a signification? You might even say that it translates internationally! There are some delicate bits in *Transition To Philosophy* that don't. So we see something approaching the sum of all difference connected; then we see something else, something devoid. And what about that black cataract over its eye? And what about the fact that it has no sound like a mute button on a remote control? I heard that language is just differences in sound combined with differences in idea; is the blot exempt? How does the blot attain meaning? How does it journey from Signification to Significance? And is it just a piece in a beautiful opera of being? And does it mean something about imminent death? Have I been sent the blot because I have been hired to die?

*****

The scene is my bedroom, the anagram of boredom. It is not a crime scene, but we can investigate. There is a nylon string guitar leaning up against the chest of drawers; there are clothes on the floor; there is a mirror; there are two portraits of John Lennon done my artist friend; there is the Tower — that instrument of philosophy — where I started with a book that began to emanate smell — and continued to collect weird books that seemed subject to natural magic. No, it is not a crime scene, just a domestic scene, but if I am being sent the blot as a death threat, it could be the scene of a crime nevertheless.

My bed is unmade. My phone on the bedside table. My tea also. A hair-band (for I have long hair.) Some defunct Vape pens. Some empty Vape juice packets. A candle left over from the recent power-cut. The bedside light is on but not the main light. The watch my friend got me for Christmas is here. Two old laptops are flat on the chest of drawers. It is Night. No music pours through the house. I turn my mind to Heaven. Heaven is a pile of imaginary statistics that no-one will ever get to see. There is fly-paper hanging down from a notch on the window. There is a waste paper basket containing old bottles, sweet wrappers et al.

I decide the best thing I can do is to take the Tower back to my old bedroom where my own bookshelves are. The books in this present bedroom are Dr. Bob's, not mine. So I take the Tower back to the other shelves and integrate the Tower into those other shelves so that no-one would notice it.

## MORE ON THE BLOT

I am thinking about the blot again, or as some call it "the dot." The blot, meaning death. Why have I been commissioned to do it? Let me not launch into paranoid conspiracy theories. Let me undress the presentation of the dot as a philosopher would a proposition. But wait, that is not possible. It is not a proposition. It isn't actual language, in not employing the mechanics of meaning, through differentiation. It differs from All Other Language in a singular way, by warrant of it not connoting, other than through the superstitious mode of it connoting imminent death. But maybe it's not so superstitious – maybe I *am* about to die?

I think mortality is a form that you can write against; that death can wake you up and get you writing for your life. But something about this blot idea, it is less an hypothetical death than ever before. It is a more accelerated, real sense of death. I think in short that God is a game. That a game is based on permutation. That even a game of cards can be a rehearsal for death. I think *The Lords And The New Creatures* is also a game – a wide, yellow circle with death the pinpoint centre and the circumference closing in. I think it also a media-compression experiment dreamed up on LSD under a hot, Californian sun.

The friend who gave me the blot: he was a poet as I was too. He had one when we were young going something like:

"A house. At night. Waiting in darkness

for you. Who do you think of when

you touch yourself in the shower?"

I puzzled over it for a long time because he did delight in a wilful opacity; and it took me years to crack the code. In fact it was the night before my father died that I got what he was talking about. So I wrote it down on my computer. Then my dad died and I think the next thing in the list was:

"Death's breath is a tear of flame,

with waxy dreadlocks drooped in shame."

They existed either side of the actual pinpoint moment of death. Now the friend has asked me to do the blot... knowing what he meant in his poem, I think again of the blot, and the way the meaning of the poem only came to me in a time coinciding with my dad's death. If you're too slow you've missed it. This friend, he didn't ideate the "intended meaning" himself but encrypted it, and applied it to music too, to beautiful effect. He made songs in other words that never repeat themselves, never look back, always move on, make you wonder "how did we get here?" miles down the line. Not that it's not but who you think of touching yourself in the shower is the one with all the wordly power over you.

## THE FACE OF STARS

How do I know the face of stars was scripted in the Bible? Firstly, we were three gathered in the name. We were on a camping holiday in Eskdale, and I had taken us to a tarn at sunset. The sun went down and we walked back through the concussive dark guided by a cigarette lighter's spark, came out of the dripping trees into the open, crossed the River Esk on the stepping stones and stood beneath the universe at the clearing by St. Catherine's Church. The universe was enlumed, drenched with electric diamonds, wet, dripping grape-bunches of stars; and Tom and I stood there together while Ben fished his fags out of the river; and we saw a shooting star or "fire fish tail" course across the Night from right to left; and we pointed, simultaneously, up at it in rapture; and all of a sudden we recognised the face of stars, there where the shooting star fizzled out; so we were already pointing up at it; and we sighed and were excited; and Ben came from the river bank and asked us what we were pointing at; and I guided his eyebeam across the Night so that he could also see it – the face of stars.

We had to walk away and did. Now the question is: how do I know it was scripted in the Bible? Well, I don't know but believe, if you may permit a difference, and this belief has been engendered by a series of random text messages I have been sent from two separate numbers, containing Biblical quotes. Maybe, you will say they are taken out of context; but reading them, with my experience, I understood that the face of stars was scripted in the Bible. The list of quotes, divided into two books according to which number the texts were sent from, is as follows…

## BOOK 1

Tue 1 Jan 2019. 00. 00

It is of the LORD's mercies that we are not consumed, because his compassions fail not. Lam 3 v 22.

Mon 26 Sept 2022. 11. 38

He maketh the storm a calm, so that the waves thereof are still. Psalm 107 v 29

Mon 10th Oct 2022. 11. 45

For of him, and through him, are all things: to whom be glory for ever. Amen. Romans 11 v 36

Mon 24th Oct 2022. 12. 02.

... that we through patience and comfort of the scriptures might have hope. Romans 15 v 4.

Thursday 22 Dec 2022. 11. 20.

In whom ye also trusted, after that ye heard the word of truth. Eph 1 v 13.

Mon 2nd Jan, 2023. 12. 47

...so loved... John 3 v 16

Mon 16<sup>th</sup> Jan. 2023. 12. 16

For the LORD gives wisdom; From His mouth come knowledge and understanding. Proverbs 2 v 6.

Mon 30<sup>th</sup> Jan 2023. 12. 16.

Come unto me, all ye that labour and are heavy laden, and I will give you rest. Matthew 11 v 28

Tuesday, 14 Feb 2023. 13. 32.

Shall not the Judge of all the earth do right? Genesis 18 v 25.

Monday 27th Feb 2023. 13. 05.

But he giveth more grace. Wherefore he saith, God resisteth the proud, but giveth grace unto the humble. James 4 v 6

Mon 10th April 2023. 11. 38

Who is wise, and he shall understand these things, prudent, & he shall know them for the ways of the Lord are right, & the just shall walk in them. Hosea 14 v 9.

Mon 24th April 2023. 13. 09.

After he had patiently endured, he obtained the promise. Heb 6 v 15.

Mon 8th May 2023. 19. 45

I am Alpha and Omega, the beginning and the end, the first and the last. Rev 22 v 13.

Mon 22d May 2023. 12. 24

by his own blood he entered in once into the holy place, having obtained eternal redemption for us. Heb 9 v 12.

Mon 5th June 2023. 12. 35

Cast not away therefore your confidence, which hath great recompence of reward. Hebrews 10 v 35.

Mon 19 June 2023. 11. 05

Behold, what manner of love the Father has bestowed upon us, that we should be called the sons of God. 1 John 3 v 1

Tuesday 4th July 2023. 12. 53

Abraham believed God, and it was counted unto him for righteousness. Romans 4 v 3.

Mon 17 July 2023. 11. 46

For thou art with me Psalm 23 v 4

Monday 7 Aug 2023. 09. 42

the LORD is thy keeper: the LORD is thy shade upon thy right hand. Psalm 121 v 5.

Mon 9th Oct 2023. 23. 18

To everything there is a season, and a time to every purpose under the heaven. Ecc 3 v 1

Mon 6th Nov 2023: 13. 24

To whom then will ye liken God? Or what likeness will ye compare unto him? Is 49 v 18.

Sunday 26th Nov 2023. 06. 22

our sufficiency is of God. 2 Cor 3 v 5.

Tues 19th Dec 2023. 10. 37.

Glory to God in the Highest. Luke 2 v 14

Monday 1st Jan 2024. 13. 25.

But blessed are your eyes, for they see: and your ears, for they hear. Matthew 13 v 16.

Monday 15 Jan 2024. 11. 12.

I the LORD.. will hold thine hand, and will keep thee. Isaiah 42 v 6.

Monday 29 Jan 2024. 12. 19.

I will go before thee and make the crooked places straight. Isaiah 45 v 2.

Monday 11 March 2024. 11. 24

Worthy is the lamb. Revelation 5 v 12

Monday 25th March 2024. 11. 32.

Or do you not know that your body is the temple of the Holy Spirit who is in you, whom you have from God, and you are not your own? 1 Cor 6 v 19

Monday 8th April. 11. 54

Seek the Lord, and his strength: seek his face evermore. Psalm 105 v 4.

Monday 8th July. 23. 54.

God is our refuge and strength, a very present help in trouble. Psalm 46 v 1

Whoever offers praise glorifies me. Psalm 50 v 23

Monday 15th July. 10. 39

For thou hast magnified thy word above all thy name. Psalm 138 v 2.

Monday 29 July. 11. 39.

And the Lord hath laid on Him the iniquity of us all. Isaiah 53 v 6.

Monday 12th August. 11. 15.

...upholding all things by the word of his power... Hebrews 1 v 3

Monday 26th August. 14. 17.

Come, see a man, which told me all things that ever I did, is not this the Christ? John 4 v 29

Monday 9 Sept. 12. 16

Behold, the fear of the LORD, that is wisdom; and to depart from evil is understanding. Job 28 v 28.

Monday 23rd Sept. 14. 03.

Pray without ceasing. 1 Thess 5v 17.

Monday 21 Oct. 10. 30.

Let such as love thy salvation say continually, the LORD be magnified. Psalm 40 v 16.

Monday 4th Nov. 10. 50

I am come that they might have life, and... have it more abundantly. John 10 v 10.

Mon 18th November 10. 00.

Offer unto God thanksgiving; and pay thy vows unto the most High. Psalm 50 v 14.

Mon 2nd Dec. 10. 19.

For God sent not his son into the world to condemn the world; but that the world through him might be saved. John 3 v 17

Mon 6<sup>th</sup> Jan. 10 35.

And God shall wipe away all tears from their eyes; and there shall be no more death, either sorrow, or crying, neither shall there be any more pain: for the former things have passed away. Rev 21 v 4

Mon 13 Jan 10. 17

Casting all your care upon him; for he careth for you. 1 Peter 5 v 7.

Sunday 2nd Feb 21. 55

Blessed is she who believed, for there will be a fulfillment of those things which were told her from the Lord. Luke 1 v 45

Monday 10<sup>th</sup> February. 11. 26

Shall he that contedeth with the Almighty instruct Him. Job 40 v 2

Monday 24 Feb. 10. 44.

And he arose, and rebuked the wind, and said unto the sea, Peace, be still. And the wind ceased, and there was a great calm. Mark 4 v 39.

Monday 10 March. 19. 38.

Let us therefore come boldly unto the throne of grace, that we may obtain mercy, and find grace to help in time of need. Heb 4 v 16

Mon. 10. 57.

Which hope we have as an anchor of the soul, both sure and steadfast. Hebrews 6 v 19.

Monday 7 April. 11. 35

Looking into Jesus the author and finisher of our faith. Hebrews 12 v 2

12. 15

...the son of God, who loved me, and gave himself for me. Galatians 2 v 20

Tuesday 20 May. 18. 21

Behold he cometh with clouds; and every eye shall see him. Rev 1 v 7

Monday 2 June. 10. 14.

Shall he that condendeth with the Almighty instruct him? He that reproveth God, let him answer it. Job v 2

# TRANSITION TO PHILOSOPHY VOLUME TWO

## JOHANNES BERGFORS

## BOOK TWO

Monday 19th Sept 2022. 10. 52

The Lord, he it is that doth go before thee, he will be with thee, he will not fail thee, neither forsake thee, fear not, neither be dismayed. Deut 31 v 8

Monday 3 Oct 2022. 12. 42.

Seek the Lord, and his strength, seek his face evermore. Psalm 105 v 4

Monday 17 Oct 2022. 12. 28.

It is God that girdeth me with strength, and maketh my way perfect. Psalm 18 v 32.

Monday 26 Dec 2022. 12. 44.

He that spared not his own Son, but delivered him up for us all, how shall he not with him also freely give us all things. Romans 8 v 32

Mon 23 January 2023. 11. 54

But be not thou far from me, O Lord: O my strength, haste thee to help me. Psalm 22 v 19.

Mon 6th Feb 2023. 12. 34.

The glory of the Lord shall endure for ever: the Lord shall rejoice in his works. Psalm 104 v 31.

Mon 20th Feb 2023. 11. 50

Even there shall thy had lead me, and thy right hand shall hold me. Psalm 139 v 10.

Monday 6th March 2023. 11. 22.

I will say of the LORD, He is my refuge and my fortress: My God; in him will I trust. Psalm 91 v 2.

Tuesday 4th April 2023. 21. 38.

The LORD is nigh unto them that are of a broken heart, And saveth such as be of a contrite spirit. Psalm 34 v 18.

Monday 17 April 2023. 10. 31.

Stand still and consider the wondrous works of God. Job 37 v 14.

Monday 1st May 2023. 13. 03.

Then spake Jesus… I am the light of the world: he that followeth me shall not walk in darkness, but shall have the light of life. John 8: 12

Monday 15th May 2023. 11. 46.

Be still, and know that I am God. Psalm 46 v 10.

Monday 29th May 2023. 11. 53

Great is our Lord, and of great power; His understanding is infinite. Psalm 147 v 5.

Monday 12 June 2023. 11. 52.

He telleth the number of the stars; He calleth them all by their names. Psalm 147 v 4.

Monday 26th June, 2023. 11. 18.

In the world ye shall have tribulation; but be of good cheer; I have overcome the world. John 16 v 33.

Monday 10 July 2023. 12. 04

I will remember the works of the LORD: surely I will remember thy wonders of old. Psalm 77 v 11.

Monday 24th July 2023. 10. 11.

And they remembered that God was their rock, And the high God their redeemer. Psalm 78 v 35.

Monday 7th August 2023. 10. 21

My soul longeth, yea, even fainteth for the courts of the LORD: My heart and my flesh crieth out for the living God. Psalm 84 v 2.

Monday 16th October 2023. 11. 41.

... for your Father knoweth what things ye have need of, before ye ask him. Matthew 6 v 8.

Wednesday 1st November 2023. 08. 39.

For thou, art good, and ready to forgive; And plenteous in mercy unto all them that call upon thee. Psalm 86 v 5.

Monday 13th Nov 2023. 11. 43.

My soul melteth for heaviness: Strengthen thou me according to thy word. Psalm 119 v 28

Monday 27th Nov 2023. 11. 48.

Therefore I will look unto the LORD; I will wait for the God of my salvation; my God will hear me. Micah 7 v 7.

Monday 25th December 2023. 12. 04.

Every good gift and every perfect gift is from above, and cometh down from the Father of lights, with whom is no variableness. James 1 v 17.

Wed 10th Jan 2024. 04. 59.

And the Word was made flesh, and dwelt among us... John 1 v 14.

Monday 22d January 2024. 12. 27

But be not thou far from me, O LORD: O my strength, haste thee to help me. Psalm 22 v 19.

Monday 5th Feb 2024. 11. 38.

And he arose, and rebuked the wind, and said unto the sea, Peace, be still. And the wind ceased, and there was a great calm. Mark 4 v 39

Monday 4th March 2024

For he hath made him to be sin for us, who knew no sin, that we might be made the righteousness of God in him. 2 Cor 5 v 21.

Monday 18th March 2024. 10. 30.

O LORD, thou art my God; I will exalt thee, I will praise thy name; for thou hast done wonderful things. Isaiah 25 v 1.

Monday 1st April. 12. 33.

The Lord is risen indeed. Luke 24 v 34.

Monday 8th July. 23. 54.

Unto thee, O my strength, will I sing: For God is my defence, and the God of my mercy. Psalm 59 v 17.

The Lords is nigh unto them that are of a broken heart; And saveth such as be of a contrite spirit. Psalm 34 v 18.

Monday 22nd July. 09. 39.

O give thanks unto the LORD; for he is good: For his mercy endureth forever. Psalm 136 v 1.

Monday 5th August. 11.43.

And whatsoever ye do in word or deed, do all in the name of the Lord Jesus, giving thanks to God and the Father by him. Col 3 v 17.

Monday 19th August. 10. 36.

Blessed is the man that trusteth in the LORD and whose hope the LORD is. Jeremiah 17 v 7

Mon 2nd September. 10. 54.

The voice of the LORD is powerful; The voice of the LORD is full of majesty. Psalm 29 v 4.

Monday 16th September. 10. 36.

When I said, My foot slippeth; Thy mercy, O LORD, held me up. Psalm 94 v 18.

Monday 30th September. 11. 15.

For thou hast been a strength to the poor, a strength to the needy in his distress, a refuge from the storm. Isaiah 25 v 4.

Thursday 17th Oct. 15. 38

And he said, My presence shall go with thee, and I will give thee rest. Exodus 33 v 14.

Monday 28th October. 11. 55.

Rejoicing in hope; patient in tribulation; continuing instant in prayer. Romans 12 v 12.

Monday 11th November. 10. 54

For the vision is yet for an appointed time ... though it tarry, wait for it, because it will surely come, it will not tarry. Hab 2 v 3.

Monday 25th November. 11. 53.

Wherefore putting away lying, speak every man truth with his neighbour; for we are members one of another. Ephesians 4 v 25.

Monday 9th December. 10. 48.

The LORD shall fight for you, and ye shall hold your peace. Exodus 14 v 14.

Monday 23 December. 12. 12.

When they saw the star, they rejoiced with exceeding great joy. Matthew 2 v 10.

Monday 30th December. 13. 29.

He taught me also, and said unto me, Let thine heart retain my words: Keep my commandments and live. Proverbs 4 v 4.

Monday 20ᵗʰ Jan 11. 43.

Behold, I make all things new. And he said unto me, Write; for these words are true and faithful. Revelation 21 v 5.

Monday 3ʳᵈ Feb. 11. 16.

Be not wise in thine own eyes. Fear the LORD, and depart from evil. Proverbs 3 v 7.

Mon 17ᵗʰ Feb. 10. 33.

If we live in the Spirit, let us also walk in the Spirit. Galatians 5 v 25.

Mon 3ʳᵈ March. 11. 19.

Peace I leave with you, my peace I give unto you: not as the world giveth, give I unto you. Let not your heart be troubled, neither let it be afraid. John 14 v 27.

Monday 17 March 11. 47.

He brought me up also out of a horrible pit, out of the miry clay, And set my feet upon a rock, and established my goings. Psalm 40 v 2.

Monday 31 March 20. 03

Hear, O LORD, when I cry with my voice: Have mercy also upon me, and answer me. Psalm 27 v 7.

Monday 11. 30

For in the time of trouble he shall hide me in his pavilion: In the secret of his tabernacle shall he hide me; he shall set me upon a rock. PS 27 v 5 TM

10. 42.


in all thy ways acknowledge him, And he shall direct thy paths. Proverbs 3 v 6.

JOHANNES BERGFORS

## "MAGIC SAYINGS HIDDEN IN THE TREETOPS"

A moocow is not made of dialectical antagonism.

Someone else can lose your marbles for you.

Vowels are our souls.

Meaning in music is solipsistic, it is faces in the fire or Hamlet's 3 creatures in a cloud-change.

Life could be a dull throb of loneliness inside your breast as well as a colourful spew going on outside the cave-walls of the skull.

If Liberalism is the allowing of all perceptions and it leads to Hamlet's harmatia irresolution, pragmatism may be the reactivation of an attitudinisation in that situation.

Planes are the shoes of clowns.

It's impossible to make a cowboy film in space.

A drum is a dream bigger than a dream of bounding in huge, magic circles in space.


The Big Mac, which contains the four basic, caveman cravings of salt, fat, sugar and protein, could be the heir to the apple of knowledge.


Love can go veggie for reasons of Disney.


Light-speed is my passport.


If acid is the microchip of a peach, the sun is the peachstone of a black hole.


It is not true that the effects of acid and of acid-rain on an imaginary species = the same, nothing, if there can be no more proof of something being real than saying it was Imagined.


The constellations only seem to turn on axis unobserved.


A trance of stalks walks on stilts like a stance on talks only to the toilet then back to bed to rest its head under the soft, Pink Panther blanket.


When a volume starts to smell of redolent flowers or Flora's perfume it could be the word of a dog.

Death's breath is a tear of flame with waxy dreadlocks drooped in shame.


When we wake words are stone shoes worn by the bottoms of clouds, weighing them down hopelessly.


It is possible to harness waves that also passed through the Beats.


Leaves that played on the surface of the water, these are the leaves they have in Heaven, these are the leaves of love.


There are fossils of art as well as fossils of life.


Connection is Heaven and Heaven connection and there is connection between Heaven and vision for vision may feel in a state of Heaven and Heaven only exist in vision.


Semantics is a road sign not a place.


Meaning is inherent in something's exact mode of expression.


Meaning is not a delusion unlike Time.

Meaning could be an emotional import given mere exo-skeleton with words.


Every planet has its own colour and 'Calliope' means 'beautiful face.'


The names of pharmaceutical medications should probably not appear in poems.


Nature is the true architecture of State.


If ever there were a light-speed law of neuroplasticity it might only be that "it is impossible to remember a new yellow line."


Cliche hurts more than truth.


Where rain falls, falling reigns.


Pictures can be done without hands.


Life is not just about naturally occurring fossils of Jim Morrison's poetry for the witness but the live Doors for everyone else too.

**Realism ice-skates on the surface of the dust.**

**Language can be smuggled out of the unconscious.**

**Enough is the hope the heart literally needs in order for it to survive without which it can stop, meaning Duff which is H suspended in deafness.**

**H20 might stand for hypothalamus tattoo.**

**Chewing gum is bi.**

**Voices only pathologise what by another name might be onjects, quavers, syllabubbles, sonic machinations at the periphery of sound, an instrument of wonder.**

**Clouds seen through hospital glass only mean that all things must pass.**

**There is no such thing as mind cancer.**

**That women like Primark is hardly a timeless idea transmitted across Time.**

Ecstasy is a teddy bear back in the garden of Eden.

Autumn is Optimus Prime already in Keats.

Freedom not poetry is the bike riding itself.

After garage and house comes library.

The poet extirpates every trace of recognition from the mind, unlooses the mind of form, method acts every adjective in 'Howl' to attain visual radio.

If your dad is an international art smuggler nicknamed Blue it can become a new sense through which you can read of future events.

It is not inconceivable that when we die we can re-access history at any point, be a real, live Red Indian, or a bird of prey soaring over a mnt.

Birds are for flying not for special perception.

The effect of global warming on the unicorn succeeded Piper At The Gates of Dawn.

The summer rain falls with as many hands as there are names for new rock bands.

The alphabet could be Nelly the Elephant's suicide note.

Sometimes on E it makes you feel like your mouth is full of cold, stunning, Heavenly, crystal water and when you speak it spills.

If form is an easel, content is a palette.

The main difference between the sticks and the city is that in the sticks you acknowledge the stranger you pass when out there walking.

Creation is a dark machine.

It's impossible to curse the sun.

Acid is a spirit-level for the spirit.

Without flaws there can be no opinions, as without imperfection there can be no taste.

Galloping water is a cool thing to say.

Things live inside onions of themselves.

Freedom flies where flags fall.

Heaven is a pile of statistics no-one will ever see.

Water's boiling point is when it starts to involuntarily breakdance to the music.

Walnut halves look like miniature, shrunken brains.

If Facebook is evil one reason is that it makes you say things you don't mean and freezes them forever.

Your right to write of who is in the shower ends where another's naked body begins.

We are hiding from *The Waste Land* in *The Waste Land*.


I prefer *The New Family Tao* to the non-fungible token.


The sound of typing can be used as percussion in non-metred Sound Art.


When Baxter the dog walks on the laptop funny things come out like the names of glitch electronica numbers.


The powers that be could be clouds that wear DM boots on their red brick road, and ripped genes adorned with peace and anarchy signs, on their protest march.


A 'tron' could be a point of intersection between technology and art or a post-poetic experiment with a psycho-technological edge.


Objects can vanish on the periphery of madness when emotions are high.


Reality is not a computer program designed by aliens in the 1980's and nor were caves alien cinemas in the long distant past.

Waiting in darkness can be nourishing for the soul, reveal a Technicolour shoal.

With drugs you have to realise: wise up or die.

The world of Stuff and Things is not amenable to the world of Transcendental Metaphysics.

Time does not pass but evaporate.

Life is naturally the opposite of Lord of The Flies because the mystic character is the one that actually does see things while everyone else thinks he's deluded.

Even a game of cards can be a rehearsal for death.

The exact same words can seem absolutely insane when written down and confer absolute genius when not written down.

Dream-meets in the silver forest, ESP and telepathy are more possible with the net around.

When it comes to the sheet where pictures grew, they could be "people," as we are people too, people who are levelled by the sheet, whose Equality is enshrined.

If you have to read Homer in order to be a philosopher everyone should have that opportunity if they choose and that is my philosophy.

Credits at the end of innocence still fall like numberless lists of fallen autumn leaves.

To be the first to coin the word "co-imagination" seems almost silly.

Crocodiles have had Sat Nav for 1000's of years before our Age.

A bird is a bird is a bird is a bird.

Just because it has been called naive to perceive of the left as a beautiful, compassionate emotion to explore doesn't mean it isn't sometimes good to go down that path.

Just because it was my brother not me that fired bullets to the top of the telegraph pole doesn't mean all statements that pertain to axiomatic truth are his intellectual property.

A thesis as thin as the Rizla it is in can lead all the way to the loony bin.


Water has no more memory than it has smell.


It is better to hide from the wind than it is to perform open heart surgery.


When I say apples "occupy" a bowl on the table, I don't mean they are a bunch of Nazis.


It would be unwise to use the same shapes as a previous writer like, for example, Jim Morrison, if your creative writing teacher says it would be unwise to.


If "Philosophy is a sterile subject" (as my friend Dr. Calculator Ptom contends) poetry is probably by default more alive.


If Flora was in nets, I'd be Barnes in the game.


Nirvana did the sheet where pictures, pictures depicting my own song lyric grew, so that's why people like it when I say it still belongs to my brother (who laid it down).

**The healing and fusing of the cassette with a pause in the song where cut and resealed in the flimsy reel in a delicate operation could be down to faith more than doubt.**


**Two photos on the blog, one for the ear, one for the eye, might still seem unfair.**


**When you get invaded by madness and hear so many voices there can seem nothing going on in your own head but straw.**


**If you did help invent the net you shouldn't have to pay for publication.**


Words appear to come out weird sometimes.


Glastonbury should be free and life like that all the time.


Some voices take a few moments to decode after their initial shocking impact.


If I said I went to the Louvres travelling by drug-hoover, it might just seem like piss.

The crawl of the Doorsian poet through modes of perception trying to find something that underlies their variability leads to water.

Maybe living here at the foot of the oldest rock I was never supposed to find out about the future that ain't what it used to be.

Cutlass maths is what I call the ruthless revisionist cut of William Carlos Williams.

We live in an Age of sending without form.

Drains can sing with Irish folk songs, about dreams that never die.

There are dreams that never die.

Love is a dream that never dies.

Even the meme has split in two, and that was the new "uncuttable" once upon a time.

There is breath in a death.

It is not necessarily a disease to not be able to cry at funerals.

The traffic lights of tears can be all dark green at times.


The impassable gulf between first and third persons has been decreed metaphysics.


The automated conveyor belt of poesis influences the voice to be a confluence of forces through voices even when I try and drive a straight line towards anywhere that may be light.


We are all in one bed in Amsterdam.


The light is a prism.


Through the Hume people come and go, Smart-talking of Ted Hughes's Crow.


Life is fast, London brutal, travelling scary.


Her wetness is so.


Angels can be as frightening as demons.


The witness was already an Irishman before Jim Morrison was born.

Voices could be the colours of the vowels and make you increase your threshold for Negative Capability.

Writing a letter Dear Music could be instructive in mental health in the future.

H does not = 0 − 0 because I have a heart.

You shouldn't put Paradise Lost to music unless it is going to be amazing so it is an aesthetic not moral question.

Isness is the centre of Everything.

Isness is the quiddity and suchness of existence.

The thing is not ideas about the thing but the thing itself.

# JOHANNES BERGFORS

## RELATIONAL DISCOMBOBULATION

I've just finished Wittgenstein's *Philosophical Investigations*. There are some interesting mirror neuron-y things in the second part; in fact I love it when it seems the structure of the book is the subtext of the examples he's discussing with intelligent selection. One thing I remembered was a game I used to play back in childhood: I would lie in bed and somehow (I forget how) with my eyes closed or else under the cover lose orientation, lose the room, forget which end of the bed my head was at, where the wall was, and how I would lie dead still and appreciate the utter lostness, the freedom from direction madly and gladly too. There was something contained in Wittgenstein's approach to an accelerated discourse combining music, geometry, psychology, maths, linguistics, and more, in the second part of his book that suddenly reminded me of the exquisite pleasure of having escaped reality in such a fashion as a kid. I say "escaped reality" but maybe that was to find it for walking on the sun as Einstein tells us there are no ups, downs, lefts or rights. This experience of having become free from knowing which way round I was lying, where the room was, where the wall was, and just lying there in incognito position I don't quite attain anymore and I can't remember the details of it that greatly as to how it was arrived at – sometimes by chance, sometimes on purpose. It's an experience of amnesia or even *ecstasia* that I mean. It wasn't a contravention of gravity but of spatial awareness; a way of escaping the obvious that would seem normally inescapable and go unnoticed too. Such an experience I would say even re-instils a belief in paradise, magic and fantasy in the young child, but that may be unqualified. To attain it again would seem too difficult. It was a relational discombobulation. A scrambling of the co-ordinates of reality.

# TRANSITION TO PHILOSOPHY VOLUME TWO

## MATHS HOMEWORK

I am reading Saul A. Kripke's fine book *Wittgenstein – On Rules And Private Language*. At least it is open on the table, if I am not actually reading in this present moment but typing. I am about half way through his discussion of how to prove to a sceptic that by the function 'plus' he means 'plus' not 'quus.' I was going to say something about not being a mathematician myself; but I did once put a + sign for an 'f' in the line

"I have a scar+ that is red and black."

It would seem I did to mathematics what my brother did to language when he came out with <BEE>. I tried the maths for the new colour as a cellular mark at seven years old. Reading Kripke's fine essay on the addition function (+) I can't help thinking I did well on that front; that my own efforts were not bad, quite interesting, even innovative. You'd have to read my seven year old text (*The Sunset Child* by John Tucker) to read a more full account.

I did also once write an album called *The Road To Heaven by Noj And The Mob*. There was also a text exploring the ideal form of defaced bank notes some time after I forewarned of September 11th in 2000. By now I am thinking more of the falsification of the Nirvana barcode: it is surely an Impossible Number. What do I mean by that? I mean that it cannot exist even though it is clearly arranged on a page as a conglomeration of ink droplets that signify, presumably, some sort of "containment of everything." We already have the sign 'Sigma' meaning the sum of all data. Quite what we need a fake and fallacious Nirvana barcode for I do not know, but we have one courtesy of a whimsical tendency in my own writing to entertain impossible mathematical functions.

Even in the cracks on the concrete floor I see writing, or rather maths, or even Logical Symbolism, like the window full of equations in the film *A Beautiful Mind*. It only takes me missing a night of sleep to be able to hallucinate whole "wall to wall occasions" as I call them (for the occasion IS the equation) in the aleatory patterns on the concrete floor.

# TRANSITION TO PHILOSOPHY VOLUME TWO

## A SYSTEMIC ERROR NEAR THE START

If philosophy be but tea I should tell you of a systemic error near the start.

My father was a life long Man United fan; but when I was very young I started to support Liverpool F. C. Their winger John Barnes was my favourite player; I had a female friend whose surname was Anfield; and Liverpool were rampant at the top of the League Table in the paper. So it seemed a no-brainer to support Liverpool; and as soon as my dad found out he came in and said:

"John, your boys are playing Arsenal today and I want you to watch Ian Wright very closely."

I was being punished: the black striker Wrighty was being used as a deadly weapon, an instrument of punishment. Moreover, as soon as I started supporting Liverpool, they stopped winning the League, and Man United took over!

There's a lesson in there for you somewhere.

I have to search my soul now and ask really deep, probing and penetrative philosophical questions such as: do you really, deep down, actually support your dad's team Man United? I think the answer to that is no, still, I still support Liverpool. But I don't follow the football anymore.


Philosophy was once decreed by Russell to be a place where science and religion meet. Science and religion both agree that behind us is Perfection be it super-symmetry of forces before Time began (to precede its own origins) or an Adamic, prelapsarian state... but that perfection is gone. Be it the Fall or be it entropy or whatever, the perfection that precedes us has been blemished. That there is a systemic error near the start has been noted on many fronts.


The point is it is too late to go back. Back is the way we cannot go. So into the future we travel, knowing Eternity is Now and Now and Now.

# TRANSITION TO PHILOSOPHY VOLUME TWO

## AN AESTHETIC ANTI-SYSTEM

If mother's flower-press ending on cannabis = a dialysis, a love poem only hoping to impress poor Flora = a motor. Well, this "florid pretext" keeps coming up. It was said by my sister Hannah that the best bit in *Transition To Philosophy* was where I argued that the dialysis extends beyond the end of the world and the emptying of space of the human form! Not wishing to copy myself, for that would be crass, I should just note that by now she is beyond me. I had a phase of writing her poetry in teenage years but it's... it's time to look back on all that folly, like Rimbaud renouncing his art. The middle aged vantage point of philosophy affords such room for reflection. If I were to ask my mother, meanwhile, what to do for a Creative Writing MA, for I did have a place once upon a time, she would say that she would make something out of Flora's "system." A point could be made here about systems which is that the very idea of a system is different in philosophy and poetry. In poetry systems are not to be trusted for they rule with fear not love; in philosophy meanwhile you hear of the triumph of so-and-so's system. I am unlikely to do a Creative Writing MA for many reasons, including funding, including mental illness, but one of my friends from a past MA course there at Lancaster also recommended me arranging my poetry according to The Florid System. By now of course I know, or rather believe, she is someone else's mating queen from the green pages of *The Lords And The New Creatures* in the flesh – so I shouldn't go there. And yet every time I think this plot is over, my mother comes in the kitchen, where I work, and gets me, say, to put some asparagus in a pint glass with water at the bottom, like a flower arrangement. Thereafter the stage is all mine and my brother's but I am tired of it now. I never got the girl on that front and so have even started to struggle to put words down about this which was once my most Rimbaudian aspect. I don't smoke cannabis anymore nor crave to sleep behind her face...

and what a beautiful face it is too. But no, alas, she is not to be mine, only in dreams. The voices whose suggestions I dare not resist say "that's just what you get when you play the game according to kinship with your little bro." Further, they say if I had shown her the maths of the new colour as a cellular mark she would've known the genius was me. The whole business is like trying to get your Undying Bitch to come, when your head is melted on MDMA, or not. Nowhere near, we start applying salt and pepper to the sauce – or mum does. Then they'll start saying my bit in the mixture was when I wrote down the voices I hear, even though they are real people elsewhere. I was the one to first articulate the pretext but by now it has been usurped and soon they'll be saying it was my mum that said it. The sauce is actually delicious, as my mother says: combining beef and gravy and sweetcorn. The potatoes are also beautiful, local, earthy, humble. Afterwards, mum says there are cherries and strawberries to finish off. So I have a handful of those. I start with the cherries, then have a strawberry, then have more cherries. They are far from running out. Who would've thought cherries could be so numinous? Now I'm onto the popcorn. It is sweet and salted mixed. I like that, possibly because the areas of the brain that deal with pleasure and pain are right next door to each other! I prefer popcorn that is mixed sweet and salty to the very sweet, almost saccharine kind. Anyhow, by now I am rambling. Soon we may turn up to the cinema to watch a film called *The Lords And The New Creatures*. Already I think they turned it into a dream rather than a film. It moved very fast and left you feel energised in the morning. Energy is good – at least positive, healing energy is. Blake said energy = eternal delight, and he was wise and knew a thing or two about life. Blake would have to be a part of the Doors computer game if that dream were ever realised; and maybe I would too. Drinking beer and smoking spliffs in the cinema has also gone under Gondwanaland by the way. Then you realise you missed out the Ketchup. Of *course* it is part of her pretext. It contains tomatoes and sugar too. There's sugar in Everything by the way, as my father saith: "reduce sugar!" he warned. He was the one that showed me said flower-press ending on cannabis: a gift from my mum to him, comprised of clippings from their Honeymoon in Crete, it came with a commentary on Taxonomic properties of the plants in terms of things like healing, food and mythological status. It was around that time, when I first read mum's "brochure," that I actually espied the woman in question trotting on a horse in the village, smirking. She's not from round these parts and the idea that someone rich would come up for holiday struck me as unlikely. So it was I felt drawn towards her: like opening my heart to find out who inside it was held to be most sacred, I fell into line. She wouldn't even befriend me on Facebook though, so you soon get the message: if someone doesn't respond to you, they don't want to talk to you. Soon enough I was writing about the tape with the pause where cut and resealed in the reel in ways I cannot remember, designing a system to do with colours and what would happen if you rewound or fast forwarded the tape. I was slow-spelling her name in this system, and rewinding and fastforwarding it too, which was but one of the beautiful things I have done that never saw the light of day. Now it is later. People said the best song in Soundcloud Rain was the one for Flora; it's my brother's one that one, even though I wrote the lyrics. I believe, that is, not only did he get <BEE> and the sheet where pictures depicting my lyric grew but he even got to know her kiss! It all makes me out to be handicapped! Soon I'll have to betray the fire-dance and rewrite the government paper I wrote at seven that helped invent the net! Then I will have pissed off people that say, hey, it's either the Doors or the State, not both. So for now I stick to the Doors. Maybe I'll find out I wasn't actually "the witness" and the Naturalistic Observations I made were done with a gun, and that the State are trying to help. Then you realise you missed out some of Nora's books… and what would they contain? Ink droplet constellations. Ink droplets standing in squad-drill formation. To not even be able to go on, when conditions are like this, so free, is a strange thing. Does one come up against a border? One comes up against an aesthetic rule: that progress should abide by an aesthetic standard, meet an aesthetic requirement; so one pauses, reflects, hears the bird song in the summer trees in the evening, drifts off, and starts wondering of cruciform pollen, how it contains mascara bruise, peacock feather, butterfly wing and velvet flare. I had hay fever as a child but homeopathy cured it. I grew out of it. I grew out of asthma too. Maybe I am growing out of poetry also; maybe what this whole "transition to philosophy" thing is about is growing out of poetry, because there is no audience; but I don't want to speak too soon. Philosophy could be air, hair, water, tea, clothes, pasta, loo-paper. Apart from a few bits and pieces it is airborne. Imagine if you could even see Flora's pretext in a painting by Delacroix. He was a Romantic, is someone I much admire... Romantic hyper-charge would be a good property, meanwhile, to invest into one's poetry. I wrote at seven that "hot July brings cooling showers/ straw berries and gilly flowers." But by now some people believe my seven year old homework is the government's! You might need running through what I actually did but I have been told by Hannah that I can't do both – both the State and the Doors. How can I lead it to the condition of tea? My brother says not to posit the same information twice; not to renew my own boyhood maths and science.

# TRANSITION TO PHILOSOPHY VOLUME TWO

## THE FRAMING OF HYPOTHESIS

The witness from *The Lords And The New You Know Who* or not would seek an hypothesis if he wished to become a philosopher. That "Barnes has scored a chicken" may be the most obvious and natural utterance but is not the right hypothesis. For one it wasn't Barnes, for another, it wasn't a chicken, for another it wasn't even a goal. Not to mention that fact that natural sciences and philosophy don't too easily mix. The witness wants his hypothesis to be as good as Barnes's goal against Brazil which is what Barnes actually scored; and yet can think of nothing more than the comic line "Barnes has scored a chicken" which for reasons as stated is spurious, specious, fallacious, wrong. Still, there are other hypotheses that are contained in his remit and his orbit: for example: it is not impossible to incrementally change the colour of white skin through mathematics: for this he would need to regurgitate his seven year old experiment into the maths of the new colour and describe why it failed to obtain the new colour. Another perhaps better option is that the face of stars was scripted in the Bible. Believing it a better hypothesis even if a bit straight, he contemplates how the John Barnes scenario would still recur in his inner monologue as he prepares for a philosophical interlude. He also assesses the extent to which none of this goes on in a world the mainstream can tolerate or picture. He hesitates before calling it "psychedelia" but recognises there is a similarity between his reports on mystic visions and the idea from Pinchbeck's *Breaking Open The Head* that psychedelia makes sense and only makes sense when you are inside it but is too easily dismissed when you are not. Attempting another hypothesis such as "existentialism is dead" would not be right either, for it would lead to no further light, be in itself dead. Of all that he has seen and done, much of which goes unreported herein, there still doesn't seem an original idea, an original hypothesis, an original theory – for that node about the Nirvana barcode is surely derived from the cover of Nirvana's *Nevermind*. So no original idea presents itself apart from, that is, his brother's notion that <BEE> might soon ensue from @ in the international language alphabet, so he must collapse into line with that. Him and his brother are not at loggerheads after all. More to the point you can recalibrate the co-ordinates of the possible without an original idea of your own. You can still be a good writer even without an original idea. To some extent originality being the first port of call means it becomes its opposite, as WB Yeats pointed out. There is, moreover, originality in the *ideal* of practising the maths for the new colour as a cellular mark even if there yields little hypothesis in a philosophical sense. Should you Google the question "can you change the colour of white skin through maths?" you will find a resounding, unilateral NO; so therein you actually might find an original hypothesis, but not one you wish to pursue, because for a start to reveal the mark that was left might incur exposure of privacy. Maybe you console yourself by now – or he does – the witness – by the fact that he showed unconscious foresight in his writing of the sheet where pictures grew? All these toys, they are not toys. All these symbols, they are not symbols but themselves. From what has been written herein I would say the best hypothesis to go with is that the face of stars was scripted in the Bible; but Millennial excitement dies down, is surpassed by an Age of Terror, which now afflicting the witness, means he doesn't even know if he is safe to mention it, said face, in the privacy of his own home, at the foot of Black Combe, with whom the stars re-align sometimes. So it is that the quest for an "abstract" for the surname goes on – and this brings us back round to John Barnes. As I stated in *Transition To Philosophy* to talk about the Morrison media-compression experiment producing results means something "kinetic" becomes something "static" – which is metaphorised as being the same thing as watching the Action Replay of Barnes's goal against Brazil. We cannot give the uncertainty back to the moment in watching the Action Replay and know the ball is going in – so something "kinetic" becomes something "static." But by now I am only repeating former writing. It does at least seem a more sophisticated "abstract" in that line, field or area than "Barnes has scored a chicken."

## JOHANNES BERGFORS

## SOMETIMES I STARE IN NUMB FRACTURE

Sometimes I stare in numb fracture at the screen entertaining much more interesting thoughts than ever get written and what would James do? He would crack the Matrix. The first thing you notice with visual radio is the swirling of colour that takes years to identify as visual radio – for you shall know it as colourful smoke before you know it as visual radio. Whether you can survive long enough to come out the other side, live to tell the tale, is a different matter.

I start to expand my compassion: to recognise, in this "maths of the new colour business" I am an annoying arsehole. So my compassion expands, EQ, heart magnetism, co-imagination, sympathy. I also don't remember what it's like to not be the witness from *The Lords And The New Creatures* or not, of which there may be more than myself, but maybe not that many more. The whole of my youth was devoted to Jim Morrison in a way. But yes, I am annoying: the + sign for the 'f' of scarf in the line

"I have a scar+ that is red and black,"

it has even been called genius by a PHD Biology student, but rereading it out of context in it can be a horror story. Originally it was innocent: I was seven. It came after spotting the flaw in the E of Einstein. But all things must pass, and I am but not bad for a right-handed gentile in the end. And the + sign may be a cross.

## TRANSITION TO PHILOSOPHY VOLUME TWO

### ON AN ORGAN

Now mum comes into the kitchen to turn the AGA up a notch. I am tempted to copy and paste in a renewal of my boyhood maths and science; but maybe sitting in this kitchen with this AGA I can go somewhere new? She makes it look like an accident – the way we are connected, in sympathy – the way proceeding with the book is contained in her action. You might get that when I used the + sign for the 'f', I calibrated an algorithm that sublimates numbers and letters on a cellular level; to see if the new colour could be rendered as a cellular mark. You might get that I left it a mere case of counting. But to repeat it herein, now that I am not seven but forty three, and to only isolate bits of it, would create something like an advert rather than science itself. To read the original you can read *The Sunset Child* by John Tucker which is my real name (Johannes Bergfors is my philosophy name.) There the experiment is offset by not even knowing what cannabis is, getting the name of the pollen wrong, so it's innocent. Anyhow the temperature in the kitchen where I now sit is quite high so I am topless; but the AGA was down a bit so we had to turn it up. I think it's raining outside. It is. And my identity is what I think of. I love to think of myself as a philosopher but there is always the identity of the beautiful minded mathematician from the past. One thing is for sure – I am glad to not copy and paste in my renewal of the government paper. Not that I am against the government. I am living in trust that on an organic level it's best done in innocence, best when I was seven. The mark was with me during my degree!

JOHANNES BERGFORS

ANOTHER ONE ON THE FLO'

It wouldn't quite be the same if I said "if an hour-glass ending on a piece of bliss could = a dialysis, a love poem only hoping not to bore her could = a motor." The thing is we live in an age where a supercomputer can put every word, book, letter, sentence, paragraph in every order – like the machine in *Gulliver's Travels* which was at the time only fictional. There are probably some exceptions, and my maths and James's <BEE> were probably once upon a time exceptions – but other than that everything is foreseen. It redefines God that they can do that. But when you deal with a flower-press ending on cannabis – I think that escapes the totalitarian machination. Computers don't chop plants into positions of collocation. Something organic is going on that is out of their reach.

Anyhow, by now Flora is out of my reach. I never got to be with her. Of all I did with my life, there were some great things, attaining the face of stars andcetera, discovering the sheet, being the witness or not, in no particular order, helping invent the net, hosting The Plough alignment, testing the edge of self-evolution with an experiment into the maths of the new colour as a cellular mark – but of all of it, I wonder if being with her would've been the crowning achievement – something I never got to know, something I never will never get to know. It would've been Keatsian to bring out a love poem book for her but was not to be. I'm not giving up, don't get me wrong, for then there would be nothing more to crow about. I'm just exemplifying my philosophy in a kitchen whose fridge pipes up and starts droning as I write. Then you realise you've missed out the Diet Coke.

ANOTHER ONE ON THE DOOR

I don't know why I made certain Naturalistic Observations as a child. It could've been my dad's business. It could've been that Jim Morrison wrote "a creature waits out the war" in *The Lords And The New Creatures* and my dad sold his art dealing business when the Berlin Wall fell. Said art dealing business might be a lie though, and his actual business may have been *The Lords And The New Creatures* itself. He may have been sponsored by some genius philosophers to use me as witness. There are several possibilities and I don't blame anyone, nor know the truth. So in these conditions, in these times, this Digital Age by now, I must relinquish my position as the scripted, definite witness. So in a way I resign, leaving the whole game to renew itself. In a way if I was the witness, I can't keep clinging to it – can accept that it's past tense. I might be doing what I think you want me to do, but that is also what I may be required to do. My curiosity as to what really happened hasn't gone away, but like Rimbaud or even Prospero I renounce. It's probably part and parcel of abjuring nursing the suffering of my ideals. Of going from idealism to pragmatism.

## POSTMODERN SELFHOOD

I always find it boring, churning out philosophical data on the area of the self. Once I drew two, large, overlapping circles, one for the Known, one for the Unknown and said the oval-shaped bit in the middle where they overlapped and clapped was the "area of the self." The idea was that as we find things out, the area expands – the known and the unknown come together – until there is a moment of eclipse.

Later I said to my philosopher friends round the table: "ask yourself "how are you?" or even "how am I?" You find there's nothing there. It's empty."

That approach to the area of the self was either derived from frying the brain on LSD and waking up alone and unreal or by existentialism – peeling back layers of falsity only to find nothing underneath.

Later still I considered that I was a net so fine-mesh it was but grey, smoke, static and fleck, neither retaining nor permitting anything. When I hung around with a true philosopher he then said those exact words to me, words I had thought, an image I had conjured, as if he had read my mind.

It works the other way too: I considered the image that I was spreading the same packet of butter over an ever-increasing surface area of toast: then I went and read the exact phrase in an Arab Strap record sleeve that came before I had thought it.

More genre-appropriate techno-jargon would be to say that the ontological excavation, the archaeological sense of self, is the same as the existential detective case, and the Plathian multiplicity of selves, and amounts to a postmodern "tumulus" or burial mound. I like the word "tumulus" when applied as a substantive corresponding to a sense of self.

You can also be in a state of unself. This word presumably derives from being "unselfish." But it has slightly different implications, not necessarily those of having escaped want, but those of having an imploded sense of selfhood perhaps. Anyhow, it is when we go beyond the realm of the self and the ego that we find the realms of art and science, as Einstein said.

In this evolving narrative of my sense of self, I started to hear voices and became mentally ill. New images for selfhood post mental illness have not been forthcoming, but I try to remain kind to all those whom I love. It's good to be kind. You should be nice to people, as my brother says. My mother is extremely nice.

## ALIEN SPACE PROGRAM

Well, philosophy. You read it and want to play the Game. You want to get involved, get stuck in, even make a lasting claim. But there's a lot of reading to do before you are qualified. I have been considering, of late, the idea that reality is a computer program designed by aliens in the 1980's. It is a variant on a theme of Russell's, I gather, from reading *Think* by Simon Blackburn. How do I know that reality isn't a computer program designed by aliens in the 1980's?

Back then I was used as a tool to help invent the net. If you've been reading my books you'll know: when someone was needed to store the idea of the net in the attic in writing in order to give it a chance to grow, it was me – and I did not know – and the book stayed in the attic all those years. That may be where I get the idea from; but how can I actually prove or confute either way the idea that reality is a computer program designed by aliens in the 1980's?

**Traditionally I would say: (a) *The Lords And The New Creatures* by Jim Morrison was published in 1969, at least I believe it was. This may only be a belief but that may have to suffice. (b) I believe my English-teaching granny on my dad's side was on this earth before I was born. You understand though that in the computer program there are "antecedents things" left to blind us. Like some people believe fossils are planted by God to test us, test our belief in the Creation story.**

ANOTHER ONE ON THE FLOTSAM ETHER

"We're soon enough in the flotsam ether," I once wrote, concluding a love poem... to still be doing this would be not right though. I don't mean writing, I don't mean searching, I don't mean the quest for meaning – I mean weeping salad. I mean that if a flower-press ending on cannabis = a dialysis a love poem hoping to impress poor Flora = a motor but seeing as I no longer smoke weed nor am in love with her anymore I can't see how this eschatological pretext is of any interest to me. So I am putting it out there like furniture on E-bay in case you want to pick it up, take it up as your cause; but don't be surprised if she being the mating queen from the green pages in the flesh does not respond to you when you contact her on FB, smitten and in empty warehouse zones of the psyche.


*ketamineguitar*

JOHANNES BERGFORS

SELF-REFLECTION

I still feel Little Miss Philosophy is the one for me even if I am not the best. I feel this would be a Third at University level, this document contained herein where in English Literature and Creative Writing I already got a First; but it doesn't matter – because it makes me pleased – and feels like the right thing to be doing. I am happy reading philosophy, sitting up in bed rather than on my side. Most of my best points already went into the first volume, *Transition To Philosophy*, but it being philosophy, the subject opens up and there is always more. I already know what I am going to try and achieve with my next book, which I shall not let on in case the subject radically changes, or my mind does. There is a lot of room for changeability in my process. I would say though it will be more of this processing of Time to trial and outcome and with a futuristic view in mind too which sees me occupied in terms of spare time continuum. Herein, I particularly liked the way the Biblical quotes blended into the "magic sayings hidden in the tree tops," because it was like breaking bread. The quest for meaning which I am involved in will surely go on into the future still. The transition to philosophy is ongoing, all about the journey, a journey of becoming, and I don't know where it will end. The resources available to me are my dad's philosophy bookshelves from London University in the 1960's, the online world where I can Google "contemporary philosophers" and buy books on Amazon, the company of my deep and left handed brother and mother, the great outdoors in the awe-inspiring Lake District, and my memory of interactions with other philosophers in time past. I also have, here at this island of humanity, voices, which can be real people, tuned in to the same thing. I can watch Youtube videos, read books, and take notes at the laptop. I am an amateur ordinary speech philosopher if I say I am for the duration of the sentence. Remembering days when I didn't know where I would get undressed or where my bones would rest each night, nomadic days, I seem to remember the birth of "philosophy chat rooms" in real rooms where real people would talk of real issues and on real drugs too. Back then the present author could be heard to say things like "existentialism isn't really regarded as a philosophy anymore because it's all about faith," but you never saw him reading *Being And Nothingness*. These days I hope the reverse is the case; that I devote my life to reading, here at the fell's foot, and think clearly before I speak, and speak clearly about what is on my mind. One problem is that I found it too hard to get my little thing about helping invent the net in because at my laptop screen it is too windy and there are too many flies. Maybe next time I'll give you a rundown of some of the main moves I made but for now I breathe a sigh of relief that we didn't incur the problem of mathematics whom it would seem could be lies, could be the language of Nature.

ABOUT THE AUTHOR

**Johannes Bergfors (which is the philosophy name of John F B Tucker) was born in London in 1982 to a Finnish mother and an English father. He got a First Class Honours degree in English, Creative Writing and Practise from Lancaster University in 2009. He now lives in Cumbria, at the foot of Black Combe, with his mother and brother.**

# TRANSITION TO PHILOSOPHY VOLUME TWO

www.ingramcontent.com/pod-product-compliance
Lightning Source LLC
Chambersburg PA
CBHW031154160426
43193CB00008B/368